Yes, I Can See

Velvia D. Norman

Illustrated by Geovanni Livingston

AuthorHouse™
1663 Liberty Drive
Bloomington, IN 47403
www.authorhouse.com
Phone: 833-262-8899

This book is printed on acid-free paper.

ISBN: 978-1-6655-0983-1 (sc)
ISBN: 978-1-6655-0984-8 (hc)
ISBN: 978-1-6655-0982-4 (e)

Library of Congress Control Number: 2020924093

Print information available on the last page.

Published by AuthorHouse 12/11/2020

authorHOUSE®

Dedication

I am dedicating this first of the five-series Yes, I Can Collection to my six grandchildren: Hope, Heaven, Naisha, Bloom, Hezekiah and Harmony. I hope it inspires and encourages them as they learn to read and identify items alphabetically.

Yes, I Can is a series of five books featuring A–Z illustrations page by page. Each book will cover one of the five senses (sight, taste, hearing, smell, and touch). The five books are intended to teach, encourage, and inspire young children to identify alphabetical words that represent the five senses as they learn to read.

A

Yes, I can see an **Alligator.**

Yes, I can see a **B**ear.

Yes, I can see a **Cat**.

D

Yes, I can see a Dog.

Yes, I can see an Elephant.

F

Yes, I can see a Frog.

Yes, I can see a **Giraffe.**

Yes, I can see a Horse.

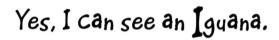

Yes, I can see an **I**guana.

Yes, I can see a Jellyfish.

K

Yes, I can see a Kangaroo.

Yes, I can see a Lion.

M

Yes, I can see a Monkey.

Yes, I can see a **Nase**.

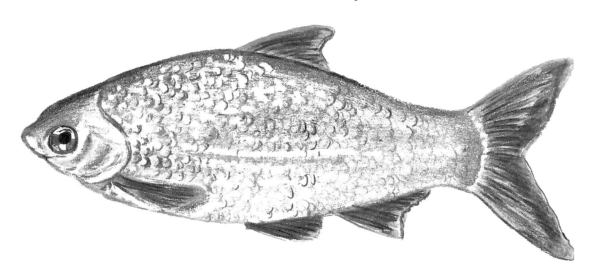

Yes, I can see an **O**ctopus.

P

Yes, I can see a **Panda**.

Yes, I can see a Quail.

R

Yes, I can see a Rabbit.

Yes, I can see a **S**quirrel.

Yes, I can see a Tiger.

Yes, I can see an Umbrella bird.

Yes, I can see a Vulture.

Yes, I can see a Wolf.

Yes, I can see an **X**-ray tetra.

Yes, I can see a Yak.

Z

Yes, I can see a Zebra.

YES, I CAN SEE

Forthcoming books in the series:

Yes, I Can Taste
Yes, I Can Hear
Yes, I Can Smell
Yes, I Can Touch

Printed in the United States
By Bookmasters